Padiham

BRITAIN IN OLD PHOTOGRAPHS

PADIHAM

JACK NADIN & DUNCAN ARMSTRONG

First published 2009
Reprinted 2014

The History Press
The Mill, Brimscombe Port
Stroud, Gloucestershire, GL5 2QG
www.thehistorypress.co.uk

© Jack Nadin and Duncan Armstrong, 2009

The right of Jack Nadin and Duncan Armstrong to be identified as
the Authors of this work has been asserted in accordance with the
Copyrights, Designs and Patents Act 1988.

All rights reserved. No part of this book may be reprinted or reproduced
or utilised in any form or by any electronic, mechanical or other
means, now known or hereafter invented, including photocopying and
recording, or in any information storage or retrieval system, without the
permission in writing from the Publishers.
British Library Cataloguing in Publication Data.
A catalogue record for this book is available from the British Library.

ISBN 978 0 7524 5188 6

Typesetting and origination by The History Press
Printed in Great Britain

CONTENTS

	Acknowledgements	6
	Introduction	7
1	Historic Halls and Rural Houses	9
2	Industrial Padiham	17
3	Transport and Getting Around	27
4	Inns and Taverns	35
5	Church, Chapel and Education	43
6	Sports and Events	55
7	Conflicts and Celebrations	63
8	Rooftops and Hidden Places	73
9	People and Places	79

ACKNOWLEDGEMENTS

The authors would like to thank the following people for their time and generosity, in particular those who gave us permission to use their photographs, without which there would be no book: Mike Townend at Towneley Hall Museum and Art Gallery and Burnley Borough Council; Padiham Archives, and in particular Ann and Bobby Clark. The staff at Burnley and Padiham Reference Libraries; Archer Lee; John Carroll, head at St John The Baptist School, Padiham; Ann Whalley of Taunton, Somerset; and Chris Speak. 'Padiham Urban District Council, Eighty Years of Local Government', a booklet by Molly Haines and Margaret Jones, gives a real insight into early local government administration. Likewise, 'Industrial Heritage: A Guide to the Industrial Archaeology of Padiham and District' by Mike Rothwell was also a great help on the chapter on local industry. Lastly, but by no means least, thanks to local historian Ken Spencer, who is always willing to help in any history project and pass on his vast knowledge of local history.

The images featured are from Duncan Armstrong's collection unless otherwise credited.

INTRODUCTION

Padiham is situated on the banks of the River Calder, three miles west of Burnley and eight miles east of Blackburn in East Lancashire. Immediately to the north lies the well-wooded Huntroyde Estate, and beyond is the Sabden Valley and Forest of Pendle, an area of outstanding natural beauty. There are several accounts of how the town of Padiham got its name:

(1)   Land belonging to the sons of Pad or Paddi of Cockersand Abbey near Lancaster.
(2)   The Roman Emperor, Antoninus Caracalla, in his progress from York to Ribchester, commented on the resemblance of the settlement with Padua, a fortified city in Italy!
(3)   A traveller passing through the village asked a cottager where he was. The occupant, an Irishman, misunderstood him and thought he asked him *who* he was, and replied, 'Paddy, I am and Paddy I be.'

By 1253 a water-powered corn mill was in existence and remained on the same site until being replaced by the Liberal Club. The first seam of coal at Padiham was recorded in 1434; a coal mine was operating in 1529 and many small pits were worked within the township, the last closing about 1870. The dominant industry by far was weaving, at first by handlooms, but by about 1790 the first mill was built – but still employed handlooms. The main period of development was the mid to late nineteenth century and by 1906 there were twenty mills working with a total of 11,600 looms.

Today, only one weaving concern still remains, employment now being gained from a number of small and varied industries – although a major manufacturer employing a workforce of almost 1,000 people at its height, producing gas fires and heaters, closed down in 2007. Communications were greatly improved when the loop railway line was built between Blackburn and Rose Grove, opening in 1875 for goods and 1876 for passengers. The station closed for regular passenger trains in 1957 and for excursions in 1963.

A chantry chapel existed in the town in 1451, which was progressively added to and rebuilt until 1866, by which time it had become unsafe and was replaced by the fine church which exists today, built in the Perpendicular style.

The town is well served with shopping facilities and the market, closed in 1956, reopened, but closed again in 2007. A good, frequent bus service exists and road communications are excellent with the M65 being only two miles away and direct access is also available to the M66 and Manchester. The visiting motorist will find the town congestion-free and all car parks are free.

Jack Nadin and Duncan Armstrong, 2009

1

HISTORIC HALLS AND RURAL HOUSES

It has been suggested that the design of Gawthorpe Hall is very similar to the work of Robert Smyson, the architect of Hardwick Hall in Derbyshire and Longleat in Wiltshire, among others. The exterior of Gawthorpe was completed in 1602 after two years work; another three years were taken up completing the interior and furnishing the hall. The Shuttleworth family have been connected with the Gawthorpe estate since the fourteenth century, and held Gawthorpe Hall until 1970, when the Fourth Lord Shuttleworth passed the property to the National Trust, although it is financed and run by Lancashire County Council. Charlotte Brontë visited Gawthorpe Hall on two occasions, and it was shortly after her second visit there that she died. On this last occasion, in 1855, she and her husband, the Revd Arthur Bell Nicholls, had visited the hall for the purpose of being interviewed in connection with the offer of a post at the church at Habergham, an offer which Mr Nicholls was obliged to decline. The couch on which the couple sat during their interview at Gawthorpe is still there. The Long Gallery at Gawthorpe is hung with portraits of important figures from the seventeenth century, some of which are on loan from the National Gallery – while several of the other rooms are decked out with needlework, costumes and lacework renown for being the next most extensive collection in the country outside the Victoria and Albert Museum, and brought together by the last member of the Shuttleworth family to live here, Rachel Kay-Shuttleworth, who died at the hall on 20 April 1967.

Huntroyde was the seat of the Starkie family for hundreds of years, but few will have actually seen it save for a photographic image or two. The hall itself was said to have been set in the finest oak timber parkland in the country – a number of oaks planted in the reign of Elizabeth I may still survive, some of them being very large. It has also been said that John O'Gaunt, the first Duke of Lancaster, built a hunting lodge where Huntroyde now stands. Originally, Huntroyde dated from 1576, and in the 1660s eight hearths were listed here. In 1777 a large extension was added in the style of the period, but was later demolished around 1963. The original house has been altered and improved over the years, fortunately in a very tasteful style.

Hargrove is down a rough track known as Guide Lane off the Padiham bypass, just before the Higham road is reached. The house was the home of yeomen farmers named Webster for over 400 years. A William Webster was living here at the time of Edward IV and in 1499 the estate passed on to his son, Richard. So it went on until 1758, when another Richard Webster died without a male heir. In 1798, Hargrove was purchased by the Huntroyde Estate. The building we see today probably dates from the seventeenth century, and the porch, although in character with the style of the house, was not the original and has now been removed. For a few years a small coal mine supplied the house and adjacent cottages with fuel from the Arley seam, the best coal in the Burnley Coalfield outcrops around here.

This fine late sixteenth to early seventeenth-century house on Victoria Road was nearly demolished after standing empty for several years in the 1960s – happily Stockbridge House was saved. We know that Richard and Jane Holt were farmers here in 1802 and that the south side of the building was rebuilt in the nineteenth century. Frederick Crossley, who was appointed to the position of land agent for the Shuttleworth's of Gawthorpe Hall in 1913, lived at Stockbridge House for practically all the years he worked for them, until at least 1945. For a short while the house was used as a private school. The Jacobean chimney was removed without permission; no action was taken initially but when the property was re-sold an amount of money was withheld in order that the chimney be restored – thankfully it was.

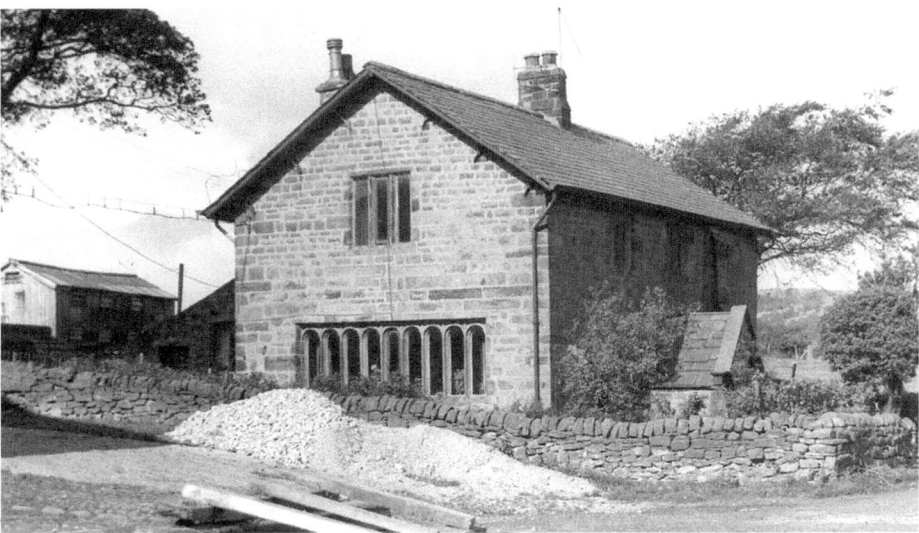

High Whitaker Farm lies between Grove Lane and the Padiham bypass. The house is sixteenth century, but must have been built before 1578, when John Whitaker was listed as being the last male Whitaker to live there. The house was used for secret Catholic meetings during the reign of Henry VIII and still retains a priest's hiding hole from this time.
The building we see today is all that remains of a much larger house – notice the nine light-moulded mullioned windows with arched heads in the gable end.

Priddy Bank Farm is down a track and public footpath across from the old Red Rock Inn on the road between Padiham and Sabden, off Slade Lane. This small farmhouse was built around the second part of the seventeenth century, though the portion of the house to the right of the picture is a roughly-built extension. The name Priddy Bank is something of a problem – it could be a corruption of 'Pretty' or it could mean 'Privy'! We like to think the former applies, in fact it is written as 'Pretty Bank' in the 1881 directory when William Sagar was farmer there. The layout of the house was altered probably at the end of the nineteenth century when a new door, unfortunately in the style of the times, was added. The original doorway to the right was made into a two light window.

If, instead of taking the lane to Priddy Bank Farm, you take the track right behind the former Red Rock Inn, the delightful Foulds House Farm will soon be reached. This fine old building has a massive outside chimney on one gable, and a double-storied porch to the front with the initials and date 'H.W. – J.W. 1677'. This stands for Hugh Whittaker (yeoman) and his wife Jennet Whittaker. The section of Foulds House to the east, on the right in the photograph, is a nineteenth-century rebuild.

Arbory Lodge on Arbory Drive has been described as a boastful extravagance to the richness of the Starkie Family, landed gentry of Huntroyde. It was built about 1790 and used to guard one of the entrance drives to Huntroyde – locally, it is known as 'T' Castle'. Alice Speak, the widow of John Speak who used to be a farm labourer working for the Huntroyde Estate, was living here in the 1860s and managed to raise her four children, Nancy, Mary, Alice and Amos, within the damp confines of the gatehouse. Today, Arbory Lodge is an enchanting and desirable private residence, which has retained many of its original features.

Stirkin Hill, on the Blackburn Road, is a former Huntroyde farm of 25 acres, though today it is a private residence. The house is difficult to date with any precision as many alterations took place in the nineteenth century. There was a remarkable incident near Stirkin Hill in August 1945; a Ribble double-decker bus on the Burnley to Preston run suddenly swerved off the road for no apparent reason and plunged down a 12ft embankment near the house. Twenty-six of the passengers were rushed to hospital with various injuries. Happily no one was seriously hurt – and more importantly no one was killed. Stirkin is a rather strange name in our modern language – it means 'a heifer or cow not yet calved'.

Craggs is off Whalley Road, and was the home in the 1880s to John Whitaker, a cotton spinner and manufacturer. He would have had full view of Craggs Colliery in a field a few hundred yards from the farm, the shaft of which can still be seen today. This old pit was finally abandoned in 1887. Craggs dates from around 1840, although it is possible that it was built on the site of a much older farm as a barn here bears the date 1777.

Isles House stands in its own walled gardens on the corner of Arbory Drive and Whalley Road. The present building dates from 1806, although it has been largely altered over the years. It was put up for sale by auction at the Starkie Arms on 17 December 1806, when 'newly erected'. William Heap was born at Isles House in 1826 – he went on to form his own civil engineering company, which, among other things, was responsible for building the huge 220ft-high big wheel at Blackpool in 1896. Other residents at Isle House have included members of the Helm family, manufacturers, and Daniel Howsin, the agent for Huntroyde. The house is gradually being restored and sash windows replace modern versions.

Higher Slade can be found down a track off Slade Lane, on the left before Pennine Grove. This former farm probably dates from the mid-1600s, for we know that it played host to Nonconformist meetings ministered by one Thomas Jollie, formerly of Altham Church, until they died out around 1688. By the 1900s Slade Farm consisted of 111 acres, and was worked by Ann Hitchon, the aged widow of Peter Hitchon. The name Slade simply means 'open space between banks or woods/a forest glade, or boggy land'.

The former Green Farm still exists on Hapton Road, which, up until 1894 and the formation of the Padiham Urban District Council, was actually in Hapton; it is a grade II listed building and dates from the seventeenth century. The attached cottage, to the right in the photograph, is a good example of an early seventeenth-century cross wing. It is the cottage that retains most of the original features, notice the huge outside chimney stack and the mullion windows. Richard Potter, who worked his way up from being a farm labourer, worked Green Farm back in 1923, and Ormerod Potter is listed as the farmer here in 1959. A small room in the roof space was discovered here in the 1970s, which may have been a priest hiding hole possibly dating from around the 1560s.

In what is left of the old church graveyard at St Leonard's you can still see the memorial to Elijah Helm of Grove House, who died on 5 June 1859 aged seventy-three years. It was Elijah, a local cotton manufacturer, who built Grove House in the year 1845. Another member of the same family, Henry Helm, was living at Grove House in the 1870s, after which the house was used by the local Methodist movement as a residence for the circuit ministers. Norman Blezard of the firm James Blezard & Sons acquired the house in 1893. Today it is used as a children's nursery, though for many years it served as offices for Lancashire Grinding Wheels, later known as Carborundum Ltd.

2

INDUSTRIAL PADIHAM

Clay Bank Mill, constructed in 1790 at the Moor Lane end of East Street, was the first purpose-built factory in Padiham, although at first it only housed handlooms. Soon other mills followed, and by the 1850s the conglomeration of factories had grown up around the Lune Street, Wyre Street and Ribble Street areas. The naming of the factories also became something of a patriotic affair – with names such as Victoria Mill, Albert Mill, Wellington Mill and Britannia Mill. Power loom weaving at Clay Bank Mill, pictured above, was only introduced in 1848 by the manufacturer George Hargreaves. By 1854, the mill was in the occupancy of Thomas Bibby, and in 1854 was advertised to let with power for seventy-eight looms – it was advertised again in 1865, this time with eighty-five looms. After 1881 the old mill ceased to be associated with the cotton trade and took on several other occupancies. These included a marine store and a foundry, and at the start of the twentieth century part of the mill was gutted by fire. Afterwards, in 1910, part of the former mill was turned into an institution, known locally as 'T' Ragged School'. This bit of old Padiham survived until 1996, having been associated with the printing trade from the 1950s. A row of new houses, Clay Bank Fold, now occupies the site.

Left: Padiham Old Mill on Factory Lane was constructed in 1807 by Henry Helm, as the datestone 'H. Helm 1807' depicts. In 1856, the mill ceased to be connected with the cotton industry, and from 1890 through to the late 1920s a furniture dealer occupied the building; later in the 1940s the top floor was used as a billiard hall. Many locals will remember the mill being Fred Pollard Textiles Ltd, a fent shop dealing in cloth off-cuts and carpet roll ends. This firm closed down after more than sixty years of trading in April 2004. It has recently been converted to flats.

Below: This picture could be any weaving mill in Lancashire, but actually it is Jubilee Mill in 1980. Notice the overhead line shafting, which drove the looms, and the cotton fluff hanging from the light fittings. The noise when all these looms were running at once was terrific, little wonder that the weavers developed a kind of mime language known as mee-mowing, exaggerating the lip movement and using hand signals to communicate with one another on the mill floor. Although the steam-driven machinery was antiquated, it provided quality cloth for Marks & Spencer.

This photograph, taken just before Jubilee Mill was demolished in March 1986, shows just how extensive the mill was. One of the last directors was David Waddington, who became the Home Secretary in the Conservative Government.

The engine house at Jubilee Mill, seen here from Green Brook, still survives and is a grade II listed building – it bears a datestone 'Jubilee Mill, 1887, The Padiham Room and Power Company'. The 800hp cross compound engine was installed in 1888 and ran until 1980, but was later removed to Matlock for restoration and preservation. The engine tenter here rested not on a stool, but a settee, and oiled the engine with a copper kettle. When the looms were electrified the steam engine continued to run half an hour a week to run the lift!

Albion Mill was known by many as Perseverance Mill, after the firm who took it over in the mid-1980s – but officially it is Albion Mill. This was the largest weaving mill in Padiham and was first started in 1905 by the Albion Room and Power Co. Ltd. The mill, which employed 205 people, went into receivership in 2005, and was demolished in 2008.

Smithygate Mill was built for throstle spinning in 1835. Spinning ended in 1871 and from around 1900 the mill was used by a variety of firms, including the Padiham Soap and Chemical Company and, perhaps best known, the Padiham Aerated Water Company, founded by Josiah Monk of Brook Foot Farm on Grove Lane in around 1898. Another well-known character was 'Jimmy Nobber' (Major Hargreaves' brother) who ran a second-hand business in part of the mill during the 1940s and '50s. The mill was demolished in 1967.

Right: Another Padiham 'pop' works was Hills Ltd, with works behind Stockbridge Road. The firm was founded by Thomas William Hill, a native of Kildwick, Yorkshire who came to Padiham around 1881. The photograph shows Ralph Whitworth operating the first pop machine at the works.

Below: Power loom weaving and the factory system evolved from the old handloom weavers. Old Moss, shown here on Higham Road, was the home to Lancashire's last handloom weaver, William Wade. He was born around 1805 in some old cottages near Cock Bridge. Handloom weaving had generally ceased by the 1860s, but William stubbornly carried on the handloom weavers' trade. It is thought that he died around 1892, but not before he took his handloom to the Manchester Exhibition and gave a demonstration there on the dying art of handloom weaving. The farm cottage still exists but is much altered, as is the adjoining barn now converted into a house.

Looking down Eccleshill Street towards the Hand and Shuttle pub, c. 1960. The three-storey building with loading bays was used for making 'Hills Specials' lightweight racing cycle frames, famed for their quality throughout the country. The building was known as the Clarion Cycle Works and employed up to twenty people at one time until closure around 1958. Later, part of the building was occupied by a joiner, M.R. Gilbert, but only for a short time as the premises were demolished a few years later. It is difficult to imagine today that a factory, a cottage and two terraced houses existed on this site.

There has been a smithy on Guy Street since the late sixteenth, early seventeenth century, although the building we see today is built around an earlier stone structure, which still exists inside, complete with mullioned windows. Dennis Haworth was the blacksmith and wheelwright here at the turn of the nineteenth century. The cottages to the left were used for many years as lock-ups, one being occupied by Irish John, a rag and bone man. Later the cottages were restored, the plans being prepared by co-author Duncan Armstrong, who also supplied authentic gas wall lights. A traditional black-leaded Yorkshire fire range was also fitted.

A lesser known industry at Padiham was mining. This image shows a tramway, known locally as a ginny, in Grove Wood, which transported the coal in small wagons from the pits to Padiham coal staithe. At first these tramways were worked by horses, and later by an endless chain system. The line of this ginny, which closed around 1936, can still be seen in Grove Wood. Previous to the ginny being constructed, a crude tramway existed following a different course in part and served the early small pits at Ightenhill. Horses would have been used to haul the tubs along.

The Cornish Beam Engine house at East Pit on Grove Lane was a vertical type engine with an iron rocking arm at the top, one side connected to the pistons and cylinder, while the other was connected with the crank arm and flywheel. The main driving shaft passed through the engine house walls where it engaged into two cogwheels. This was connected to two wooden arms, which in turn connected with two rocking iron cradles, which controlled the rams on the 15in delivery pipes. The engine could be run on as little as 8lbs of steam pressure supplied by a 9ft-diameter single flue Cornish boiler. East Pit on Grove Lane dated from at least 1706, as depicted on the datestone above the old drift bore. At the bottom of the East Pit shaft were three tunnels, all stone arched. One went towards Brookfoot Farm, one towards High Whitaker Farm, and the third towards Hargrove Farm. An old water delivery course taking the water from the workings at East Pit was all stone arched and had a datestone 'J.S. 1839'; the initials stand for 'Janet Shuttleworth'. (English Heritage)

Above: After leaving Grove Wood, the ginny travelled along Partridge Hill and eventually arrived at the Coal Staithe, now a car park and formerly Padiham market, almost behind the old Liberal Club. The unflanged wheels on the tubs tell us that they ran on L-shaped rails (a section of which survives), and in the groove on top of the wagons rested the endless chain, which hauled the tubs along.

Left: Thought to have been the largest excavator in Europe, 'Marion' was used by Wimpey, contractors to the National Coal Board on the Grove Lane Opencast Site, seen here in September 1961. 'Marion' had neither wheels nor tracks, but 'walked' on huge feet. Many old coal workings were revealed during the excavations, including a large area of charred coal. Investigations revealed that in the distant past cattle with foot and mouth disease were thrown into the old workings and set alight with paraffin, this in turn set fire to the coal.

James Blezard came to Padiham around 1840 to work as a joiner and wheelwright – and went on to become a major employer in the town. He started a foundry near the old market in Clitheroe Street in 1859, and in 1869 moved to Guy Fold. Later, in 1890, the firm was able to purchase the Victoria Mill estate and operated from there until comparatively recently – but only to supply fittings to the plumbing trade.

Richard Smith's cabinet and school furniture works was at 51 Burnley Road, on the corner with Darwen Street and Eccleshill Street, a site now occupied by the car park belonging to the Hand and Shuttle pub. Richard was a Padiham lad born and bred, and lived at 89 Windsor Terrace on Church Street. In the early 1880s he employed five men and three boys at the works. By the mid-1940s this building had become a butcher's shop belonging to James Wilkinson, and later it became Sager's butchers, before it was demolished in 1973.

Padiham corn mill was recorded as being in existence as far back as 1253. This view of the mill building, which was rebuilt many times over the centuries, probably dates from sometime after 1814, when a fire gutted the mill and claimed the life of one Matthew Wilkinson. The corn mill was water powered, taking water from the River Calder which ran in a 'goit' and returned back to the river behind the present-day Padiham clinic. The tenant farmers of Charles Towneley at Hapton were obliged by the term of their lease to grind their corn at Padiham corn mill. During the Cotton Famine from 1861 there was great distress in the Lancashire mills as the American ports were blocked – depriving the Lancashire mills of raw cotton. Sir James Kay-Shuttleworth opened a soup kitchen and working men's club at the old corn mill to try and relieve some of the distress. In 1870, Sir James handed over the club to the Padiham Liberals. The Liberals prospered and in 1897 announced the building of a brand new club on the site, thus bringing to an end the old Padiham corn mill. In its place was built the present fine building, which opened on 28 April 1898 on Burnley Road, and is now used in part as Padiham youth club. (Padiham Archives)

3

TRANSPORT AND GETTING AROUND

The opening of the North Lancashire, or Great Harwood Loop in 1876 revolutionised the movement of people and goods. This atmospheric image shows engine 42898 as it struggles up Padiham Bank towards Rosegrove, near the bridge over Green Brook, with coal empties from the power station. At 1 in 40, this gradient was one of the steepest in the country and assistance was often required, as depicted here with exhaust from the banking engine seen in the distance.

'Wakes Week' at Padiham station was eagerly awaited by the multitude of workers as they all lined up to wait for the steam engine to pull in and take them to Blackpool and the coast. Adverts for Player's Navy Cut cigarettes, Whitbread's London Stout and Swan Vestas Matches on the advertising boards tell of the habits of the day.

This view of Padiham station looking towards Rosegrove was taken pre-1922, this being the year the Lancashire and Yorkshire Railway was taken over by the London and North Western Railway. 1957 saw the closure of the station, together with Simonstone and Great Harwood to regular passenger services, however 'holiday' trains ran mainly to the Lancashire coast until 1963. The following year the track was lifted. Between Padiham and Blackburn, however, the 2-mile section to Rosegrove remained open to serve the power station until around 1993, though it took another sixteen years to lift the rails.

This heavy goods engine, no. 90420, built during the Second World War, was busy shunting wagons near Padiham station goods yard sidings in around 1960. The large building behind the engine was the goods shed.

The steep bank running down towards Padiham Power Station was the scene of a number of runaways, like the one shown in this photograph. A thousand tons of steel wagons full of coal takes some holding back! A short section of the old main line was retained to allow trains to run into ballast without causing too much damage.

This little engine taking the coal empties from Padiham in 1959 entered service on 27 February 1890 and lasted until November 1959 before being scrapped. One example of these little locos has been preserved on the East Lancashire Railway at Bury. They were simple but successful locomotives, and in their younger days were regularly used on ten-coach express trains to the Lancashire coast.

An electric tram outside Padiham terminus some time after 1902, its destination Nelson. A horse-drawn tramway was first opened in 1881, soon replaced by steam and then again by electricity, before finally being replaced by buses in 1935. What is now the hardware shop on Burnley Road used to be the tram office, and the building on the right is the Co-op grocery department, which was replaced by a new store in 1974.

Above: There was evidently some sort of celebration going on around 1898 on the old Padiham Bridge going by the large crowds seen here in a photograph taken from the window of the Bridge Inn. The old steam tram trundles its way across the bridge through the crowds, hauling a two-decker bogie trailer. (Towneley Hall Art Gallery and Museum)

Right: These 'chubby' little single decker buses were first introduced in 1952. They were well liked and successful, lasting until the mid-1970s. BCN no. 44 is seen here passing under Dryden Street Bridge on its last day of operation in August 1976. Almost all the buses in this group have been preserved.

A single decker Leyland 'Royal Tiger' returning from the Sabden run negotiates what is still a busy junction with Church Street, Burnley Road and Moor Lane. The buildings on the right-hand side are Webster's Buildings, named after the family who built them in 1878. Behind that is the Masonic building on the right of Moor Lane. Each doorway here has a triple lintel over the top.

This ex-London Routemaster bus, built in 1965, was one of a group bought by Burnley and Pendle. Here it makes its way up Burnley Road in 1988. It was the last of the old rear end open-platform buses with conductors to be used in the area. Although over twenty years old, they still provided a fast service.

This horse-drawn cab makes its way through Dryden Street Bridge sometime after the building of Albion Mill in 1906, which can be seen in the background. Cab proprietors at this time included Chadwick Bros (and fish dealers) at 7 Green lane, and James Roberts on Station Road.

This leisurely form of transport taking the bride to St Leonard's Church in 1985 was provided by Bernard Bond, who lived at the old smithy on Guy Street. He also used it to collect his wife from work at Morley's in front of hundreds of workers.

This view of Whitegate Garage looking along Cowley Crescent has changed a lot since it was taken in 1973. The buildings to the left were used to house Central Motors coaches – earlier in the 1950s it was used as a depot for the Nationalised British Road Service lorries.

4

INNS AND TAVERNS

Padiham had an amazing number of alehouses and pubs for a town of its size, there are references to no less than forty-three over the years. The Old Black Bull was the oldest hostelry in Padiham before it closed down in 1938. The present building dates from the seventeenth century, but it probably replaced a medieval structure on the same site. In around 1868 part of the inn was used as a butcher's shop, as seen here. Thomas Eccles and his wife Sarah ran the pub in the early 1880s – the couple were married next door at St Leonard's Church in 1874. For many years after its closure the building was occupied by Houston and Forbes, architects, though today the much-altered building is a restaurant.

The Starkie Arms is another old Padiham inn, seen here in the distance, although it has been greatly altered over the years – this was the main stop-off point at Padiham for post and stagecoaches. The inn was advertised to be let in 1842 with 'Good stables, Coach House, Cow House, Barn and Other Outbuildings, and Several Closes of Rich Meadow of about 24 Acres'. The landlord then was John Waddington. It was not unusual at this time for landlords of inns and taverns to also work land attached to the inn – in fact many old inns started life as farms. Notice too part of the old Swan Inn on the right. (Towneley Hall Art Gallery and Museum)

Across from the Starkie Arms is the King's Arms, seen here in 1985, which is named after King George IV (1762-1830). The inn, first mentioned in 1824 during King George's reign, was kept by Ellen Anderton. An 'Arms' is simply a meeting place. The New Black Bull next door dates from around 1834, and a building here mentioned in 1824 may have been known as the 'Clock Face Inn'. It was in a cottage on Calder Street, to the right of the King's Arms, that the Padiham Co-op was established in 1869.

The Cross Hill Inn, sometimes known as the Cross Hill Tavern, stood at 1-3 Bank Street – the buildings still survive and are now private houses. At the time this photograph was taken, around the early 1880s, the landlord was Thomas Gunson Robinson, but it ceased trading around 1902. The inn was a Thwaites house and it is interesting to note that Daniel Thwaite, the Blackburn brewer, also had hunting and fishing rights down to the River Calder. (Towneley Hall Art Gallery and Museum)

The crowd get ready for the Whitsuntide Walks from the Commercial Inn on Church Street in 1914. The inn was known locally as 'T' Bottom Drum' as, when the weather was bad, the band would abandon their part and nip into the pub rather than continuing up to 'T' Top Drum' (Whalley Range). The big bass drum, too large to go in the pub, was left outside. In August of this year, the bloodiest conflict in human history was about to start. (Towneley Hall Art Gallery and Museum)

The Whalley Range is seen here in 1978. Known as the White House from 1887 until the 1890s, it is still known by locals as 'T' Top Drum'.

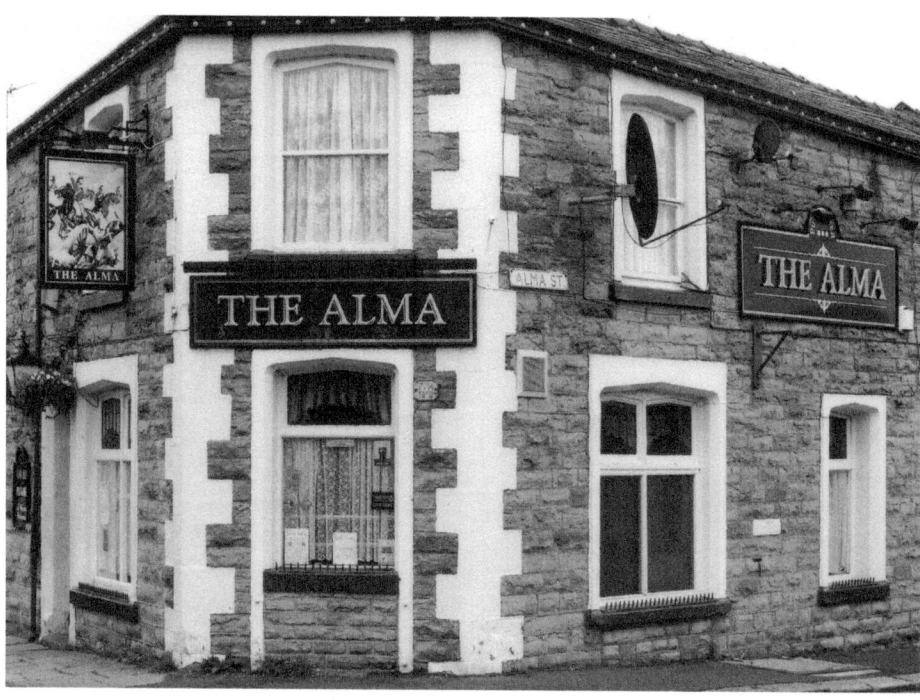

The inn sign on the Alma depicts a scene from the Battle of the Alma (20 September 1854), often considered the first battle of the Crimean War. However, the pub is not mentioned until the late 1870s. The walled-up doorway on the corner of the building is the original entrance to the inn. There was yet another pub at 26 Alma Street (now a private house) known as the Partridge Inn, which finished trading in about 1896.

The Hare and Hounds, showing the three cottages known as 'Bloater Hall' that used to stand in front of the inn. Notice that two of the cottages have what are called Yorkshire Sash windows on the upper floor – these slide horizontally rather than the more traditional up and down. The inn is unique in the area for its unusual outside steps into the pub. In January 1888, the local newspaper reported that, 'A very enjoyable evening was spent at the Hare and Hounds, when the landlady Mrs Whitehead gave her customers their Christmas treat. The pianist Mr Luther Helm got to work immediately and songs were rendered in good style by Mr Kay and Shane Snowden.'

The Free Gardeners at 2 St Giles Street, seen here in 1983, is named after the United Order of Free Gardeners, a friendly society. Laurel Lodge, a Padiham branch of the Free Gardeners, was established in 1827. Sixty years before this photograph was taken, the building above the Free Gardeners was the busy grocer's shop belonging to Jimmy Hargreaves, but by the time this photograph had been taken it had recently been vacated by Alf Thompson, electrician. There was a strange incident at the pub which happened to a tramping wheelwright, William Burns, in 1897. William, being of fine voice, was asked to sing some songs by the regulars – this he did, but after the third song he fell down dead for no apparent reason. St Giles Street is still referred to by old Padihamers as Club Street, a number of houses being purchased by an early form of co-operative mortgage.

Higher up St Giles Street and on the opposite side from the Free Gardeners was another alehouse, the Volunteers Arms, named after the Rifle Volunteer Corps which was formed nationally after 1859 and the Crimean War. The pub was demolished soon after this photograph from 1956 was taken, the landlord's name over the door being H. Hudson.

This shop at 19-21 Moor Lane, now a private house, used to be the Joiners Arms in the 1880s and '90s. The landlord here was William Wade, who died in 1890 and is buried in Blackburn Road cemetery. Perhaps Kate O'Toole, an unmarried weaver, had been drinking here back in 1887. A constable had to pick her up several times on Ightenhill Street. Telling her she would be reported, Kate replied, 'I'm all reight, it's not me that's drunk, it's mi' legs that's drunk.' Nevertheless, Kate was fined 10s plus costs.

This building on Tattersall Street in the town centre, shown here in 1984, used to be the Orchard Inn. Luke Taylor, who was the landlord here in 1876, was summoned for having his house open outside the permitted hours. He was fined 40s and costs and ordered that his licence be endorsed. At the time this photograph was taken the building was being renovated – but work suddenly stopped and soon after it was demolished. A semi-detached dwelling has now been built on the site.

The Bridge Inn, seen here in October 1978, is happily still with us, unlike a number of other Padiham pubs. The inn takes its name from Padiham Bridge, an important crossing of the River Calder. The pub probably dates from around the late 1850s, when Padiham was expanding on this side of the river. It was also used as the tram waiting room in the late nineteenth century. It is interesting to note that at the back of the Bridge Inn on the 1844-48 OS Map there is marked a 'rope walk' where the strands of rope were laid out before twisting into the rope itself. There was also another, later rope works in Padiham known as the Mount Pleasant Rope Works, which was in Slade Lane near the present Hargrove Avenue– this was run by Margaret Myers.

The Victoria Hotel dates from around the same time as the Bridge Inn, and is of course named after Queen Victoria. In July 1888, one of the 'new fangled' trams was making its way down Burnley Road towards Padiham Bridge when it jumped the metals and dashed across the road, striking the Victoria pub. Fortunately no one was injured, but some damage was done to the corner of the building on the Burnley side, which can still be seen to this day. The Victoria Hotel closed in late 2008, and its future looks in doubt at the time of writing.

Regulars at the old White Horse Inn on Burnley Road appear to be getting ready for the annual pub trip. The papers they are holding says: 'The White Horse Wizards'. Now, who were they, we might wonder? The name of the landlord over the pub door is Jack Barrett. (Padiham Archives)

5

CHURCH, CHAPEL AND EDUCATION

A chantry chapel existed on the site of the present-day St Leonard's Church as far back as 1451. Between 1520 and 1536 a new church was built with a square tower; this was rebuilt in 1766, although the tower was retained. A hundred years later the old church was demolished, as seen here, and a new church built in the Perpendicular style to a design by William Waddington of Burnley. On 13 May 1866 the very last service was held in the old church to a large congregation. There was little thought given to health and safety in those days – look at the workmen knocking the walls down beneath their very feet, and the man on top of the church tower! Older Padiham residents still talk of the church as 'Thowd Peg' for some obscure reason. The font, which is still in use, was presented to the church in 1525 by Abbott Paslew, the last Abbott of Whalley Abbey. The original market was held around the church, as were the punishment stocks, recorded as being used in 1858 for Sabbath Breaking. The man being 'punished', however, declared that he rather enjoyed it if anything, as he got lots of rum and tea whilst he was in it, 'which he would have missed if he had been out'. (Towneley Hall Art Gallery and Museum)

Little has changed at the present-day church of St Leonard's, save for the wall being taken back slightly to allow for road widening. At the east end of the nave is a brass to Thomas Yate, 'servante to the right worshipfull Richard Shuttleworth 34 yeares', who died at Gawthorpe on 30 May 1643, whilst in the chancel is a beautiful marble tablet by the sculpture John Gibson (1790-1866), a memorial to Le Gendre Starkie who passed away in 1822. The few memorials that do remain in the churchyard can be found to the rear of the church, and include other branches of the Starkie families.

Green Church, or S.S. Anne and Elizabeth Church on Hapton Road, is an outpost of St Leonard's Church and was built at a cost of £2,000 on land given by Major Starkie of Huntroyde. It was built to a design by Stevens and Robinson of Derby and had seating for 250 persons. The rather unusual dedication is believed to have come out of respect of Major Starkie's sister, Anne Elizabeth Hortin, who died in 1869. The church still exists, although it ceased to be a place of worship in 2003, and has now been converted into residential usage.

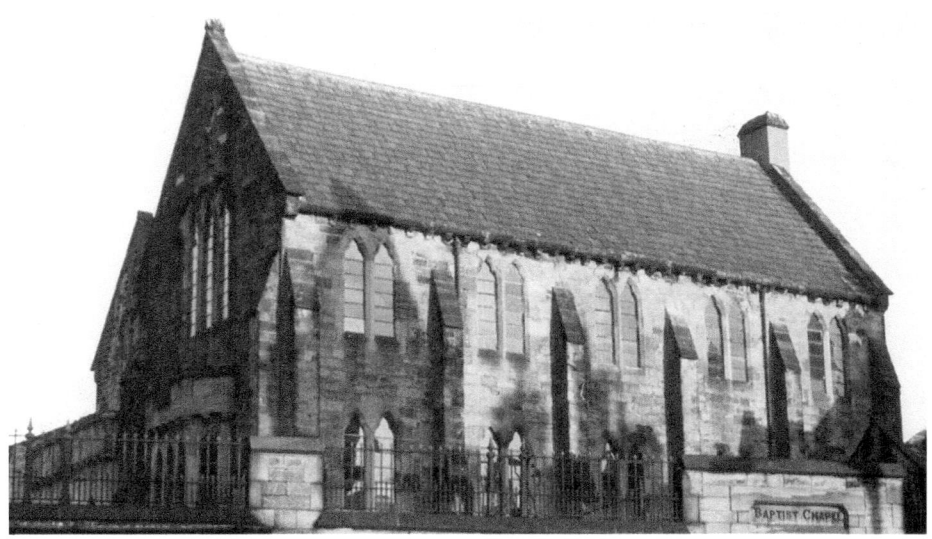

Opened in 1846 at a cost of £4,000, Burnley Road Baptist Chapel, a branch of the Sabden Baptists, could accommodate up to 450 people. In 1890 a new infant school was built next door (to the right of this photograph), which catered for 120 children, and on the spare land in front of the chapel four shops and a warehouse were built. The chapel itself was demolished in 1971, although the archway, the top of which can be seen here, was retained, together with the shops, and the old school was converted into a private dwelling.

Baptist Chapel, Pendle Street, was formed by a breakaway movement from the Burnley Road Baptists in 1866, after first using the assembly rooms on Guy Street. Around 1870 a new chapel was opened in a tinner's workshop on Morley Street, and seven years later they were able to purchase land on Pendle Street for their new place of worship. On opening, in 1877, the chapel became known as Mount Zion – it closed in 1948 and became the Co-op warehouse until 1970, when the Burnley Road Baptists moved in. This two-storey addition was added in 1892.

Cross Bank Chapel, built in 1892, was an outpost of the Church Street Wesleyan Chapel and was constructed at a cost of £3,200. In 1969 the congregations amalgamated to become known as Trinity Methodists and this resulted in the closure of the Church Street chapel.

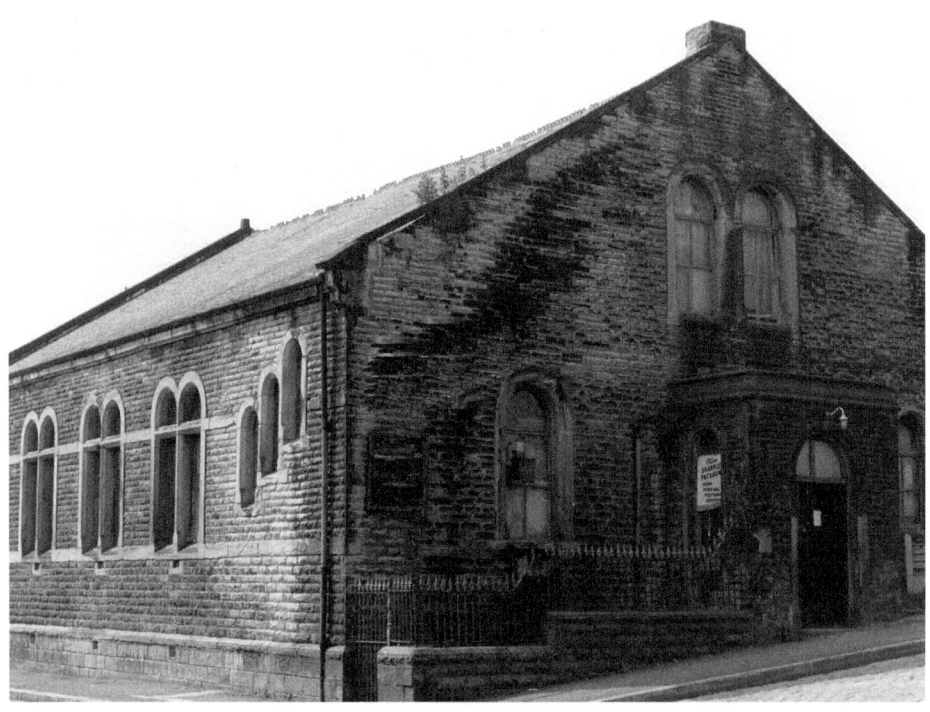

The Primitive Methodist Chapel on the corner of Hill Street and Thompson Street still survives, but is used today as a nursery. The foundation stone was laid in March 1883 at a cost of £1,800, and the chapel had seating for 500 worshippers. For many years it was the headquarters of the St John's Ambulance Brigade; the town's ambulance was also based here.

On Victoria Road we find another former chapel, which has seen a number of uses since it closed. The Horeb Union Chapel was built in 1896, as the date stone tells us, at a cost of £2,000, following a split from the Burnley Road Baptists. Today it is used as a nursery, but other uses in the past have included a driving centre and 'T' Dole'.

The Wesleyan Chapel on Church Street was built in 1847 at a cost of £3,038 with seating for 946 worshippers, later increased to 1,200. The chapel closed in 1969, was demolished in 1972, and was replaced with the 'Mews' in 1982/3. The old burial ground off North Street was landscaped in 1952, some of the headstones being placed against the wall.

Methodists were established at Padiham in 1748, two years later meeting at a small cottage on West Street. In 1779 this chapel at Hall Hill was built, which continued as a place of worship until the opening of Wesley Chapel on Church Street in 1847, when the Hall Hill site was sold off. By 1883, the building was bought back and retained as a Mission until it was demolished in 1955.

The Unitarian movement has a proud past in Padiham, being started here by the Revd Joseph Cooke in 1806. Services were held in a cottage on 'Th' Back Lane' (West Street) until this purpose-built chapel was erected in 1822. It continued to be used for religious purposes until 1874, when the present commodious building was opened. The old building was then put to use for industrial purposes, and was for many years occupied by a chemical company manufacturing size for the textile trade. This photograph shows the back of the chapel shortly before demolition in 2000 – the date stone was rescued and can be seen in the grounds of the new chapel. A newly-built house now occupies the site of the old chapel.

The fine new Unitarian chapel on Church Street near the Memorial Park was built in 1874, replacing the old chapel of 1822. The chapel, seen here in a pen and ink drawing by co-author Duncan Armstrong, is still going strong, the hall and school rooms being constantly used for various activities.

This building on Ightenhill Street is thought to have been converted from a foundry to religious use around 1807, and may have been used by Henry Helm before Padiham Old Mill was constructed. This photograph from 1982 shows the building after the Pentecostal movement vacated the premises in 1980. Afterwards it became a car showroom and garage, and at the time of writing (2009) is used by an electrical contractor.

The Kingdom Hall of Jehovah's Witnesses was located at the former Crown Hotel on Bank Street when this image was taken in 1984. A decade later and they had moved to new premises on Higham Street, which was built, it was said, in two weekends.

The building of Padiham's first national school, seen here on the left at the bottom of Mill Street, took place in 1830, the population of Padiham at the time being just 1,300. It replaced the old grammar school of 1680. The National School was extended in 1861-2, while the master's house to the rear was built in 1849. The school closed down after being condemned by the Board of Education in 1903, the pupils being transferred to the new St Leonard's School in 1905. In 1868 the school was attended by 155 children. Two years after closure the building was purchased by the Co-operative society, who built over the school yard to Burnley Road, but left the yard to Mill Street intact. When the Co-op vacated the premises it lay empty for several years and was threatened with demolition. However, it was purchased by a bedding retailer in the nick of time in 1981.

The site of the new St Leonard's School was given by Edmund Starkie JP, and the building opened on 13 April 1905. Here we have class 3 A/B in 1950. Back row, from left to right: Headmaster and form-master Mr Robert Hughes, Donald Hope, Brian Gamble, Donald Moore, Raymond Holdsworth, Derek Holland, Harry Denson, Ronnie Hoole, Amos Sedgwick, Harold Lord, Alan Rostron, Denis Hampson. Front row: Alan Hardacre, Myra Chadwick, Marion Warren, Mary Lawless, Jean Riding, Marlene Foster, Alice ?, Jenny Wilkinson, Kathleen Harling, Margaret Williamson, Jean Stacey, Jimmy Pilkington. The two girls sitting at the front are Ann Davies and Grace Starkie. (Padiham Archives)

The County Primary School on Burnley Road was opened by the Padiham Urban District Council in July 1910, on land purchased from Lord Shuttleworth at a cost of £2,789. The collection of officials at the event can be seen here. The school was built to replace Cross Bank School, which was then rented out to the Wesleyans – although Cross Bank did come back as part of the Council School later. After leaving primary school the pupils spent two years at Cross Bank before returning to the senior side of the Council School, which helped alleviate overcrowding. The style of the County Primary School is typical of the day, with gable end entrances, one for the boys and one for the girls, and has enclosed playgrounds complete with iron railings.

The first school at Partridge Hill was for infants, opening in 1858 under the directorship of Sir James Kay-Shuttleworth, when upwards of 250 people sat down for tea in the open air on a grass plot fronting the new school. After tea a meeting was held at the National School, with Sir James P. Kay-Shuttleworth, Bart, occupying the chair. Sir James later provided a girls' school in 1870, and boys' classes the following year. From 1870 the school became known as St Matthew's School, having been associated with the church of that name, also known as 'The Iron Church', which was built in the same year. The school is seen here in September 1971, shortly before demolition.

Padiham Green School opened in October 1875; the foundation stone for the new infant school was laid on 28 October 1911 and opened by the Bishop of Manchester in July 1912. This was the sad sight that greeted headmaster Paul Stamp when he returned from holiday in early August 1991. A few days before, a fire had almost completely gutted the old school. Like the Phoenix from the ashes though, a wonderful new school grew from the charred rubble, which was dedicated by the Bishop of Blackburn on 20 January 1995.

St John's Roman Catholic School is in fact the oldest Padiham school still used for its original purpose – although for many years it was in Hapton. The foundation stone was laid in 1888, and was officially opened on 26 May 1889 after 'being approved by Her Majesties Education department as a place suitable for day school teaching'. The school was built with stone from Read Quarries, with corner stones from Yorkshire quarries, at a cost of about £7,000, and had accommodation for 210 pupils. A number of additions and alterations have taken place over the years, but St John's still retains the quaint 'village school' atmosphere and is held in great affection by pupils past and present.

It was a wonderful red-letter day for Padiham when the new Technical Institute, properly 'The Victoria Memorial Institute' in memory of Queen Victoria who died in January 1901, was opened on 30 October that year. It was built on land donated by Sir Ughtred Kay-Shuttleworth, who also gifted £1,000 towards the building fund. The new institute was the envy of many other east Lancashire towns – for instance Burnley didn't get its equivalent purpose-built municipal college on Ormerod Road until 1909. 'T' Tech', as it was known, also housed Padiham's first library, which opened here in 1929. In April 1995 the former Padiham 'Tech' was closed down, and was demolished in 2001. (Padiham Archives)

We finish off this section on schools with a final look back at Gawthorpe High School, which closed its doors for the last time on 30 June 2006 to be replaced by the brand new Shuttleworth College in 2008. Gawthorpe High School was opened in 1967 by Mary Wilson, the wife of the then Labour Prime Minister, Harold Wilson, and had a capacity for 745 pupils. It provided the education for senior pupils, who had previously attended the council and St Leonard's schools. When the school was closed down an unusual situation arose when nineteen bats, which had made their home in the old school, had to be 're-housed' in purpose-built structures before demolition could begin.

6

SPORTS AND EVENTS

The *Burnley Advertiser* announced the formation of a cricket club and football club at Padiham in its November issue of 1878 – thus came into being Padiham Football Club. The ground at this time was besides the River Calder, and the team soon acquired the name 'Caldersiders' – although they are perhaps better known today as the 'Storks'. In 1882 the team won the Lancashire Cup, and in 1884, with an attendance of 9,000, beat Burnley FC 4–2. In 1916, during the middle of the First World War, the club folded, and lay dormant until after the Second World War, when the club was resurrected with the opening of the Arbories Memorial Sports Ground in 1948. The Arbories ground was dedicated as a memorial to those who perished in the Second World War. Here is the team of 1948/9. Back row, from left to right: Paul Nyland, Keith Alexander, Eric Alexander, Roy Wagner, Ronnie Smith, George Marsden. Front row: -?-, Des King, Kenneth Hanson, Bob Parkinson, Doug Smith, Ronnie Lott. The club went on to become founder members of the North West Counties Football League in 1982, but left in 1990. After spending an enormous £300,000 on upgrading the Arbories Ground in 2001 they returned to the League, and finished in the top four of the second division in 2003 and 2005. The 2009 season saw them promoted to the first division. (Padiham Archives)

Another post-war team at Padiham was the Padiham West End Club. This is the 1950/1 team. Back row, from left to right: J. Hope, S. Howarth, A. Lord, B. Taylor, B. Kay, R. Hope, J. Greenwood, B. Fielding. Front row: R. Crawford, F. Dandy, D. Burton, J. Simpson, E. Binns, H. Parker. Seated in front is Mascot J. Hope junior. (Padiham Archives)

St Matthew's Football Club were members of the Sunday School League 'A' Division, and for three successive seasons (1922/3/4) they won the Burnley Sunday School Challenge Cup, and on three different occasions won the Burnley Sunday School Hospital Cup. They were also three times champions of the League ('A' Division). Back row, from left to right: J. Cronshaw (Committee), A. Starkie, W. Starkie, E. Stevenson, L. Horsfield (Captain), E. Kelly, H. Cronshaw (Committee). Front row: A. Bridge, K. Oates, H. Starkie, C. Howarth, J. Georgson, A. Wood. (Padiham Archives)

The Britannia Wanderers football team outside their pub with their 1969/70 trophies. Back row, from left to right: David Turner, Dave Forrest, Stephen Bond, David Monk, Peter Helm, Kevin McKenna, Eddie Jackson. Front row: Keith Large, George Lum, Michael Searle, Brian O'Hara, Robert Alderson. This photograph is particularly poignant because four of these lads (Stephen Bond, David Monk, Peter Helm and Michael Searle) sadly perished in the Spanish air disaster of 3 July 1970, when their plane crashed into the Montseny Mountains, killing 112 people. (Padiham Archives)

Here we have the St John's Roman Catholic School cricket team, who won the 1950 schools knock-out competition. Back row, from left to right: Peter Alexander, Bill Locket, Martin Lambert. Middle row: Kieron Conlon, Shawn ?, Keith Pickering, ? Stockton. Front row: Terry Whitehead, Tom Conlon, Anthony Fairclough, Ian Wrigley, Keith Alexander. (Padiham Archives)

Billiards was a very popular game in Padiham, and indeed many other east Lancashire towns in the 1920s through to the 1960s. This team from the Constitution Club were the winners of the Padiham and District Amateur Billiard League for the 1935/6 season. Back row, from left to right: G. Barton, W. Livesey, J.J. Thomas, J. Monk. Middle row: E. Hall, A.C. Sherburn, Dr J.W.J. Forsythe, W. Dewhurst, T. Ward, J. Mitchell. Front row: T. Hartley, W. Blezard, H. Howarth, R.E. Adams, A. Ridehalgh.

A proud day for John Harrison as he shows off the Livesey Cup which he won in August 1969 at the Padiham Green on Park Road. The Cup dates from 1925, when William Livesey, a UDC Chairman who also ran the reed works in nearby Whittaker Street, now Park View, organised a bowling competition, and presented the winners with the cup bearing his name. (Padiham Archives)

Here we see Bob Clark, now a local councillor and ex-mayor of Padiham, aged nineteen in 1960, the winner of an Olympic title. Bob was already the Lancashire and Northern Counties bantamweight weightlifting champion, when he added the British Olympic Championship to his belt in London. Bob, weighing in at just 8st 9½lbs, managed to lift 465lbs to gain the Olympic title. (Padiham Archives)

The Padiham Clarion Cycle Club at its annual presentation meeting at the Victoria Hotel at Padiham in 1936. Cycling was a particularly popular pastime in this era, enabling the workers to get out into the countryside and enjoy the fresh air after the stuffy confines of the mills and factories. Clarion House (meaning to proclaim loudly), from which the club took its name, still exists between Newchurch and Roughlee and remains a popular meeting place for ramblers and cyclists. When the Independent Labour Party was formed by Robert Blatchford in 1892, local cyclists distributed leaflets and newsletters for the cause, and once the party had become established Clarion Houses were built throughout the country to reward their efforts. Changing leisure patterns caused a gradual decline of Clarion Houses, and today the only one left in the country is near Roughlee. (Padiham Archives)

Amateur football teams invariably played on the Fenny Fold Playing Fields off St John's Road – this match dates from 1964. An earlier and very successful boys' team was named 'Spenwell Utd' after the streets where most of the lads lived, Spenser Street and Cardwell Street.

Children from St Matthew's Sunday school, all in their best togs, pose for the camera on Padiham railway station while on a trip to Southport in 1934. (Padiham Archives)

Opposite above: 'Village Weddings' appear to have been a peculiarity to Padiham, the cast of which can be seen here at Padiham Town Hall. To mark an occasion, in this case the Jubilee Celebrations at Albion Mill in 1950, the players would all dress up and enact a wedding which would include the vicar and the bride and groom. This was all done for charities such as the St John's Ambulance and the Padiham Fire Services. A real wedding cake was baked for each performance, and then raffled off for the charities. The stage production consisted of the 'wedding', which was a comedy performance, followed in the second half by a concert by local artists. (Padiham Archives)

'Cotton Queens' were popular in the 1930s and '40s, and were used to bring a bit of glamour to the industry, and of course promoted the cotton trade. Here we see 27-year-old Barbara Melvin, Cotton Queen for 1933, in Ingham's Mill yard at their Albert mill, where she worked as a weaver. She was later selected as the Burnley area contestant for Cotton Queen of Great Britain – not bad for a working lass! A number of events were also held at the Town Hall, including one performance of the long-running national wireless show 'Have a go Joe' hosted by Wilfred Pickles (1904-1978). In fact the very last show was held at Padiham Town Hall at Wilfred's request; he often passed through the town on his way to Blackpool, but never stopped here. One day he said, 'I will stop to visit the town,' and he did, for the very last show. (Padiham Archives)

To be Sold By Auction.

On Thurſday the 19th Day of May next 1785. At the Houſe of Mr. Tickle in Padiham, at 5 in the afternoon in Two Lots, purſuant to Conditions to be then there produced.

Lot I. ALL that Meſſuage and Tenement called *Northwood*, near *Padiham* aforeſaid, conſiſting of a Capital Manſion Houſe, with Two other Houſes, Two Barns, and other convenient Outbuildings, and Eighteen Acres or thereabouts of rich Arable Meadow and paſture Ground, at 7 Yards to the Perch, now in the Poſſeſſion of Mr. *James Roberts* or his undertenants.

Lot II. A Meſſuage Farm and Tenement called *Sadlers*, ſituate near *Newchurch* in *Pendle* in the ſaid County, conſiſting of a Meſſuage, Barn, and other Buildings, and 50 Acres of Land or thereabouts, of the Meaſure aforeſaid, now in the Occupation of *Ellis Nutter* at the Annual Rent of £28. 7. 0.

The above Eſtates are Copyhold of Inheritance, Fine ſmall and certain.

For particulars apply to Mr. W. ROBERTS of *Hunterholme*, or Mr. H. GREENWOOD of *Burnley*.

A poster advertising the sale by auction of Northwood Farm and outbuildings near Padiham, and Saddlers Farm near Newchurch in Pendle, in May 1785. Interestingly, both farms are still with us. (Towneley Hall Art Gallery and Museum)

7

CONFLICTS AND CELEBRATIONS

The Padiham and Hapton Local Board firemen turned out on their processional float to celebrate Queen Victoria's Golden Jubilee on 21 June 1887. No doubt they would have passed under the Triumphal Arch the town folk had erected across from the National School. Besides the celebrations, beacon fires were lit all over the land, including Pendle Hill, Longridge Fell, Whalley Nab and Peneghent. Pendle was supplied with 15 tons of coal from the Cliviger Coal Co., a large amount of timber from Drews Lowerhouse printworks, and the Lancashire and Yorkshire Railway provided railway sleepers for the event. (Towneley Hall Art Gallery and Museum)

This float was getting ready for Queen Victoria's Diamond Jubilee celebrations in 1897. It was altogether a grand affair. 'No finer sight had ever been seen in the town than the open-air service in front of the church. When properly formed the procession was two miles long, with over 4,000 persons in it, along with 150 horses.' Afterwards, a treat was given at the National School for the elderly in town, where upwards of 450 people turned out. One aged fellow said that he was eighty-seven years old and declared that he 'had also browt his lad with him'. The 'lad', it emerged, was sixty-one years of age. (Padiham Archives)

The Padiham Volunteers also played an important part in the Diamond celebrations. A report stated: 'The Volunteers, some 75 strong, were under the command of Captain Bear, which, on leaving the sacred edifice (St Leonard's Church) played the National Anthem.' We can even name most of the soldiers. Back row, from left to right: Sergeant Clegg, Sergeant R. Wiggin, Sergeant Mullander (RAMC), Colour Sergeant R. Thornton, Colour Sergeant Instructor Didloe, Sergeant P. Nessler, Private G. Worral. Front row: Corporal W. Southworth, R. Wiggin (boy), Lance Corporal J. Chippendale, -?-, -?-, Cecil Didloe (boy), Corporal J. Mahon. (Towneley Hall Art Gallery and Museum)

The scene on Church Street during the Diamond Jubilee, after the open-air services were over and the processions began to move through town. Note the fine 'Gawmless' type gas lamp, an advantage point for a fine view on the left-hand side.

It was a whistle-stop tour of Lancashire for King George and his Queen on 9 July 1913 and Padiham, as always, put on the best show for them by erecting, according to the local press, 'the prettiest decorations in the district'. After touring Colne, Nelson and Burnley the royal couple had lunch at 1.10 p.m. at Gawthorpe Hall before moving on up Church Street towards Clayton-le-Moors and onto Accrington. Here is the scene soon after the royal party had passed through town, around 2.37 p.m. The group of men coming towards the camera appear by their blackened faces to be colliers, and were probably making their way home from Calder Pit having missed all the excitement. The sign on the church reads 'A Gradely Welcome Fro Thoud Foulks' (A grand welcome from the old folks). (Padiham Archives)

We are not quite sure when this image was taken – it is evidently some sort of carnival float being pulled by a fine Shire horse, and judging from their dress, it may be a celebration of the end of the First World War. We do know that it was taken outside the Railway Hotel on Station Road. (Padiham Archives)

The whole country celebrated the Silver Jubilee of King George V in 1935 – in Padiham's case this was done by tree planting by the school children in Memorial Park. The council asked all the children at schools in the town to vote for their favourite girl and boy, who then planted a tree for the occasion. Revd Roy Packer gave us this first-hand account of the proceedings in September 2008: 'I was at Padiham Council School then, when Amy Grimshaw and myself were voted the most popular couple. We were both nine years old at the time. After the event we were photographed and it was made into a postcard – I still have the original copy seventy-three years on.' (Towneley Hall Art Gallery and Museum)

Whit Walks, as a tradition, goes back generations in Padiham, and attracted crowds from near and far – maybe one incentive was due to the pubs being open all day? This image from around 1941 shows the Whit walkers making their way towards Padiham Bridge, passing Morley Street. The children, some of whom are carrying gas masks, were kept in line by holding on to a sturdy piece of rope. (Padiham Archives)

Time for more celebrations, this time for the present Queen's Coronation in 1953. Street parties were held throughout the land to celebrate the event. Here, a group of children at one such street party in the town sit down to a meal of all things 'good' for them, including ice cream, jelly and custard, cakes and sandwiches. (Padiham Archives)

Another Coronation street party, this one at the back of St John's Road – one cannot help thinking that this one was slightly more orderly and disciplined. There was live television coverage of the Coronation and many rushed out to buy or rent television sets – those that couldn't afford them were invited into the homes of those who could. (Padiham Archives)

The Padiham Unity Club Prize Jazz Band appear to have enjoyed dressing up as well as playing to the crowds. The Unity Club was on Morley Street and was also known as 'T' Bottom Club'. (Padiham Archives)

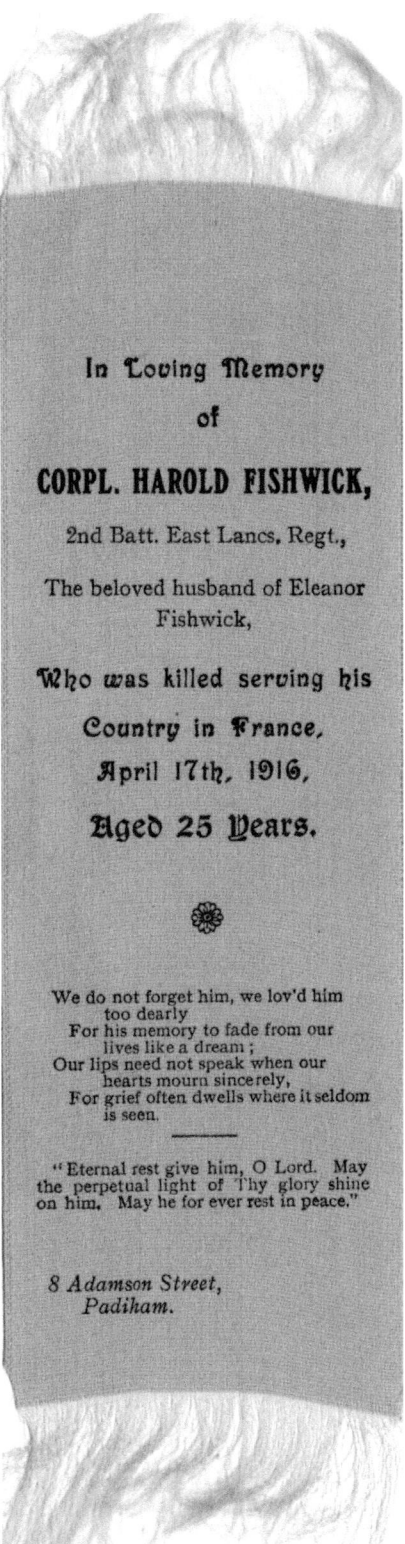

Corporal Harold Fishwick of Padiham was just one of Britain's many thousands of men and boys who never returned to their homeland during the First World War. News of his death came in a letter to his widow in a rather blunt way from his commanding officer: 'Your husband was unfortunately killed on the evening of 17th inst. At the time he was acting as a servant to me, I was with him a few minutes of him being hit. He was one of the very best, and both my platoon to which he belonged and myself join with sympathising with you in your very sad loss.' (Towneley Hall Art Gallery and Museum)

The townsfolk, in particular the women of Padiham, were quick to respond to the appalling deaths that took place in the Great War. To this end a new park was opened in 1921, mainly from the funds bequeathed by the late Thomas Clayton, this new park was named Memorial Park and dedicated to the fallen of the First World War. Padiham suffered as much as any other town in Britain in the war, and perhaps more than most. For instance one family lost no fewer than four members in the atrocities. You would be pushed to see this view, looking towards the Unitarian chapel today, as it is obscured by mature trees.

Another memorial to those who perished in the wars was the bandstand in the park, which opened in 1927. This was a popular venue at the time, and folk frequented the park on warm summer days to listen to the music of the brass bands playing. However, the bandstand burnt down and today only the rubble foundation stones of the base remain. (Padiham Archives)

This delightful, yet sad, image captures a little girl placing a floral tribute on the Padiham War Memorial, perhaps in remembrance of her father, uncle, or even her brother. Officially the memorial is known as 'The Padiham Women's Memorial Cenotaph' and was opened in October 1921 at a cost of £1,100 by Rachel Kay-Shuttleworth, daughter of Lord Shuttleworth. The heavy rain that day only added more gloom to the sombre occasion, as each of the 322 names inscribed on the monument were read out – heroes gone, but not forgotten.

URBAN DISTRICT OF PADIHAM

UNVEILING
——— ON THE ———
CENOTAPH

OF THE NAMES OF THE MEMBERS
OF HIS MAJESTY'S FORCES FROM
PADIHAM WHO GAVE THEIR LIVES
DURING THE 1939 — 1945 WAR

BY THE

Hon. R. B. Kay-Shuttleworth
J.P.

On SUNDAY, SEPTEMBER 14th, 1947

AT 3-0 P.M.

Left: The fifty-three names of those who perished in the Second World War were added to the Padiham War Memorial in 1947. Again the opening ceremony was performed by Rachel Kay-Shuttleworth, who tragically lost two brothers in the First World War and two nephews in the Second World War. As the names were finally unveiled the 'Last Post' was sounded, and slowly the British Legion banner bearers dipped their flags in a proud salute to all their fallen comrades.

Below: The Padiham Home Guard worked as factory workers, gas workers and labourers in the Second World War, while those too old to enlist played their part in the protection of the country. The Padiham branch of the 'Dad's Army' is seen here 'on T' Rec', now the site of the present-day Padiham baths. The building on the right is Padiham railway station. (Padiham Archives)

8

ROOFTOPS AND HIDDEN PLACES

This view towards Moor Lane (top centre) was taken from the tower of St Leonard's Church around 1905. In the foreground can be seen part of the old churchyard, while top left is St Leonard's National School, which appears quite new, and part of the Clay Bank Mill dating from around 1790. The only properties remaining today are houses in Gawthorpe Street (bottom right), Bank Street (left to right) with a bit of St Leonard Street (extreme left) together with St Leonard's School.

A later image from 1977, lower down Moor Lane, taken from the same vantage point atop the tower of St Leonard's Church. The Masonic Hall (the large building to the left of Guy Street) is still with us, as are the rest of the properties.

Immediately behind the church is the crowded and cramped housing belonging to Church Lane and Havelock Street. Part of the old church graveyard can be seen bottom right, whilst in the top left-hand corner is the Free Gardeners Inn. By standing at the back door of the bottom house you could touch the back of the other house in Havelock Street – these properties were cleared in the 1970s.

Looking down Mill Street, again from the church tower, the 'castellated' chimney stack (bottom left) belongs to the Starkie Arms, next door is the British Legion, now a private club, while beyond the cottages, slightly projecting, is the School Master's House, and finally there is the old National School, which, for about seventy years after closure, was part of the Padiham Industrial Co-operative Society. A glimpse of the old Globe Theatre can be seen on the right-hand side.

The large building in the centre of this photograph, taken in 1977, is the Oddfellows Hall in North Street; beyond that is the roof of the former Cross Hill Tavern and to the left of that is Trevelyan House, a building of some antiquity. Beyond, top centre, is the vacant land of the former Wesleyan chapel and school, soon to be developed as flats for the elderly.

Looking over industrial Padiham with the spire of All Saints' Church at Habergham on the horizon and Mill Street in the bottom right-hand corner – while in the opposite corner is the 'Top Bank'.

A hotchpotch of unplanned outhouses, backyard walls and former privies are shown in this scene, which still survives within the Mill Street 'Island'. Back in 1938 a master plan was devised to bulldoze most of the town centre, including this view, which would have been replaced by a dual carriageway. A year later war broke out and the plan was shelved. Happily, at the time of writing, this plan still has not been resurrected, and this charming 'secret' place of old Padiham remains.

Yet more outside privies and crowded narrow alleyways behind the Masonic Hall on Moor Lane and the houses on John O'Gaunt Street, since demolished. Little, if any, planning went into the construction of these working-class houses, many of which were within a 'hop, skip and a jump' of the mills and factories where the tenants often toiled six days a week.

A typical backstreet scene in Padiham taken in 1979, in this instance the back of Hambledon Street. A car park now occupies this site. Is it an image of gritty, northern, terraced, working-class housing, and perhaps a scene that Laurence Stephen Lowry might have appreciated?

9

PEOPLE AND PLACES

Padiham Bridge, widened on both sides in 1904, is depicted on this postcard of 1905, which was addressed to a Miss March of Skelmersdale. The caption on the back reads: 'We have landed alright about half past five. I am going to the mill tomorrow. Write back.' No one really knows how long Padiham Bridge has existed on this site. We do know that in 1457 Sir Thomas Walton bequeathed 14s towards the building of Padiham Bridge, and in 1647, when in 'a state of collapse', it was repaired at a cost of £10 at a burden to the parish. The bridge was also the place for one of this part of Lancashire's greatest hoaxes. It was just after Padiham races finished for good, way back in the mid-1850s, that the local business folk began to worry about loss of trade. To this end, some of the local wags got together and decided to publish a poster advertising a great event in town – one that was sure to bring in the crowds ... (Towneley Hall Art Gallery and Museum)

Padiham Wakes!
UNPARALLELED FEET!

MONS. SIGNOR PROFESSOR DE LA UNSINQUE,
FROM THE VILLE AQUATORIUS,

Has the distinguished honour to announce to the Admirers of the Wonderful, that he will repeat his Aquatorial Experiment (as performed at the Royal Baths of Gottenburg,) of

Walking on Water,

On MONDAY NEXT, on the RIVER CALDER, at PADIHAM :—

The Water to be taken a little above the Bridge, at 4 o'clock P.M., and, Mons. Signor Professor De la UNSINQUE's Valet will attend to receive the Offerings of the Visitors.

M. S. P. DE LA UNSINQUE IS WEB-FOOTED!!!

The Professor will afterwards take a Drive on the River, in his Aquatic Equipage—

DRAWN BY GEESE!!!

N.B. The Geese will previously Parade the Banks of the River.

... In fact a copy of the poster still survives and is reproduced here. On the day of the great event the crowds poured into town, especially those from the neighbouring town of Burnley, who were always keen to 'see owt for nowt' even if it did mean walking the three miles to Padiham and the three miles back. Everyone gathered on the banks of the Calder and waited for the event to be performed, and they waited, and they waited, but nothing appeared to be happening – apart from the ducks swimming about on the river. It was then that some bright spark realised that Mons. Signor Professor De La Unsinque must be a duck! They had all been duped – the crowds roared with laughter, the pubs filled to capacity, and a good time was had by all, until the Padiham folk started to jibe the Burnley folk for walking all that way just to see ducks walking on water. Once the Burnleyites realised that they had been tricked, near riots ensued and shutters were speedily put up on windows. Another version of the event is that the professor did arrive and actually walked across the river without getting wet – he went across the bridge! Since that time, Burnley folk became known as 'Burnley Watter Walkers' (Burnley Water Walkers), a nickname that still survives to this day, although for many years it was a risky thing to mention 'watter walkers' to Burnley folk.

It is believed that this group of gentlemen at the opening of Churn Clough Reservoir near Sabden in 1892 are members of the Padiham and Hapton Local Board – at last Padiham had a decent water supply. Long before this, when Padiham was a mere hamlet, the only source of water was from freshwater springs or wells. However, some of these springs, especially those on the Bank, lacked iodine and caused those who drank from it to develop swollen neck glands, a condition not unlike mumps. Consequently, Padiham folk acquired the nickname of 'Padiham Thicknecks'. At least that's one explanation, but there are two others. Another is that the term came from an onion presented at the Padiham Agricultural show, which had an unusually thick neck. The third was that Padiham folk are thick from the neck upwards! The authors prefer the first version! Whatever the reason, Padiham folk were quick to use their thick necks to their advantage, in particular the local colliers who bought chewing tobacco which at that time was measured by length around the neck – well you can guess who had the last laugh.

Padiham Town Hall was the scene of civic pride when it was first opened on 26 February 1938, having been built to a design by Bradshaw, Gass and Hope of Bolton, who, incidentally, also designed Stretford Town Hall. The new Town Hall, built on the site of the 'Wonder Mill', is seen here shortly after opening. Notice the tramlines and the stone setts on Burnley Road – even though the tram service had succumbed to the buses in 1935. Little has changed at Padiham Town Hall, a listed building, and it still retains much of its Art Deco interior and the charm of that era. (Padiham Archives)

The 'Wonder Mill', properly Bridge End Mill but so-called because of the Wonder Cotton Mill Co. who ran the factory in 1924. Local sarcasm dictated that it was named Wonder Mill on account that it was a wonder it ever made any money, or that it never burnt down. It was later demolished to make way for the present town hall. The mill on the right-hand side is the former Orchard Mill, which may have started life as a brewery in 1852. It was short-lived though, and closed down in 1856.

A nice view looking up from the bottom of Mill Street. On the left can be seen the stump of the Smithygate Mill chimney, and the tatty looking building and hoarding just to the right of that was once part of the Urban District Council's Health Department! The old National School had at this time been taken over by the furnishing, footwear and clothing department of the Co-operative Society.

Lodgers at Joe Miller's lodging house at 25-27 Guy Street pass the time on a warm summer's day around the early to mid-1950s. Thirty years previously, the lodging house was owned by John Thomas Waddington, who lived at 21 Moor Lane. All the properties in this picture have now been demolished.

Two ladies find time to gossip on the landing off Mytton Street in the 1950s, on what appears to be another warm summer's day. The street running across the end is Eccleshill Street, and turning left here would have brought you to the Hand and Shuttle pub and Burnley Road. The cottage right of centre appears to have been of some antiquity, but, along with all the other properties, was demolished in 1969.

Looking down Eccleshill Street before demolition in 1969/70. The white building in the centre used to be the Croftwell Inn before it was referred for compensation back in 1908, after which it became a private house, until it too was demolished.

An image of Padiham now long gone is depicted in this scene of Bank Street, around the 1920s or '30s. On the immediate left is what used to be the Cross Hill Tavern at 1-3 Bank Street, a building which is in fact still with us – as is the former Oddfellows Hall in the opposite corner. The lowly type cottages in the centre of the picture would be worth a small fortune if renovated today, had the demolition men not moved in.

This little row of shops at nos 51-55 Burnley Road, beside the former Liberal Club, was demolished in 1973, the site becoming the Hand and Shuttle car park. The shop on the left, which was finally a butcher's, contained a fine pair of bow windows. Previous use includes a smithy and, later, was occupied by Richard Smith, a cabinet-maker. The hoarding is advertising Player's No. 10 cigarettes (with coupons) for 3s 6d a packet – remember those?

Horne Street ran parallel to the River Calder and Burnley Road, and was a short street of terraced, working-class houses dating from around the 1850s. The houses were demolished around 1962, and the site was redeveloped to become the new White Horse public house. The Town Hall can be seen at the end of the street.

A carnival event wends its way along Station Road towards Green Lane. On the extreme left is the police station. Behind the horse-drawn cart, displaying the words 'Ye Olde English Garden' on it, is the Railway Hotel.

The absolute despair on the children's faces in this photograph says it all, but although we know it was taken in Padiham, we are not too sure about the occasion. The caption on the placard is difficult to read, but we think it says: 'The Padiham Section of the Burnley (Miners?) Association Distress Committee, the children assembled for their midday meal at the Unity Club, PADIHAM'. If it is 'miners?' then given the style of dress, it might be the Timber Strike of 1911?

The Unity Club, also known as 'T' Bottom Club', appear to have played an active part in times of distress during strikes and short time at Padiham. There is a little sarcasm in this image, although the subject is far from funny. The caption reads: 'Waiters; Soup Kitchen; Unity Club'. But of course there is nothing on the plates for them to wait on for! These postcards were probably sold at a penny or halfpenny each to boost the funds of the soup kitchens.

Upstream on the River Calder from Padiham Bridge is this footbridge known as Bendwood Bridge. The idea of a footbridge here was first conceived as far back as 1900 to save the weavers and factory workers the long walk round from this side of town. The first bridge was finally constructed in 1930 at a cost of £850; it was demolished in January 1984 following structural damage during flooding and was replaced by the present structure which was acquired second-hand from Penwortham, where it spanned a railway.

The effects of the disastrous floods in 1964 can be seen here at Shakespeare Street Bridge over Green Brook. The photograph was taken from the Shakespeare Hotel car park. In the background is the Albion Mill and to the left is what is now a Bertwistle's bakery branch store, formerly Shakespeare Street Co-op.

At first glance little appears to have changed in this image of Burnley Road, but the Co-op was still there, as was the old wooden bus shelter outside the Town Hall. This was plagued by vandalism and demolished in 1983 to be replaced by a metal shelter and road widening. (Towneley Hall Art Gallery and Museum)

Rachel Kay-Shuttleworth (1886-1967) was the last member of the family to live at Gawthorpe Hall and actually died there. Her legacy was the nationally important embroidery, lace making and textile collection, which can still be viewed at the hall, second only to that held at the Victoria and Albert Museum in London. Rachel was particularly skilled in the art of embroidery, and was keen to share her immense knowledge of the subject with others through examples of her work. (Towneley Hall Art Gallery and Museum)

Members of the volunteer ambulance service parade on Park Road, near where Padiham baths are today – in the background is the Banks, or 'Bunk' as it is known locally. Lord Shuttleworth of Gawthorpe Hall was keen to show his support for local groups such as this. To this end he donated two vehicles to be used as ambulances – one was a Rolls-Royce, the other a Daimler! (Towneley Hall Art Gallery and Museum)

Park Road appears to have been a popular spot for 'posing'. Here we see Ernest Bradshaw, a local tripe dresser leaning on his Model 'T' Ford. 'Ernie' later became a local Conservative councillor. At one meeting he was rambling on somewhat when a Labour councillor stood up and said, 'Do you know what, Ernie Bradshaw? Tha meks tripe, tha sells tripe, and tha talks tripe,' much to the amusement of the council members.

Major Hargreaves (Major being his Christian name, not a military title) was often considered to be the 'father' of Padiham Urban District Council, having been connected with it for over thirty-three years. He was also often called the 'Weavers Champion' and strove on many an occasion to fight their cause. Major was the son of George and Rachel Hargreaves (a marine store dealer) and died in his seventy-third year at his Garden Street home in April 1947. His brother, who was a well-known Padiham character named 'Jimmy Nobber', ran the second-hand business in part of the Smithygate mill during the 1940s and '50s.

One of Padiham's best known chip shops was Fred Manders' 'chippy' on Ingham Street, which had one of the very last coal-fired ranges in the country. Fred bought the chip shop, which still exists, in 1920 for the princely sum of £95. Fred, the 'uncrowned king of the fish fryers', ran the chippy with his wife Isabella for fifty-seven years until his retirement in 1977. (Padiham Archives)

Padiham's oldest family-run butcher's in Padiham is Charles Speak's shop on Church Street, founded in 1932. Charles Speak, seen here, was the son of a farmer from the Whalley area, who had previously been working as a butcher in Blackburn – but a few days after marrying his wife, Edith, he opened the shop on Church Street. When Charles died in February 1986, the business continued to be run by his son, Alan, who was actually born at the shop. Today, the shop still thrives under the care of Alan's son, Chris Speak. (Chris Speak)

George Rotherham ran the family firm of Rotherham's Sweet, which operated from premises on Moor Lane under the Masonic Hall. George was a great Conservative, and in 1947 stood for and won the seat for the Clay Bank Ward – a position he held until 1951. In 1951 he represented the Whitegate Ward, and in 1956 was elected to the Chair of Padiham Urban District Council. Among other offices which George held were President of the Padiham Male Voice Choir, a member of the Rotary Club, manager of Padiham Council School, and a Director of the Padiham Building Society – quite a remarkable man!

Opposite above: Burnley Road has hardly changed at all in the 100 years since this photograph was taken, save that is for the cobbled road surface and the gas lamp. The buildings on the right-hand side, 4-8 Burnley Road, are known as Hanson Buildings. The Craven Bank, on the left, had premises here as early as 1868, and by the 1890s Alfred Popplewell was manager – he lived at Isles House. The bank later became Martins Bank, which in turn has become Barclays Bank.

Opposite below: This busy scene of the Whitsun Walks was taken around 1910, near the junction of Burnley Road and Station Road. In the background we can see Ashworth's shop, known to all Padihamers, but at this time Enoch Ashworth was trading as a hatter and hosier at 30 Burnley Road – only later did he take over the shop above and take on the trade of tobacconist, which many will remember. Enoch started up on his own around 1901 at 103 Burnley Road, which is now part of the Abbey bank. The shop to the left was Harrison's grocery shop, which was demolished in 1912 to make way for the widening of Station Road. (Ann Whalley)

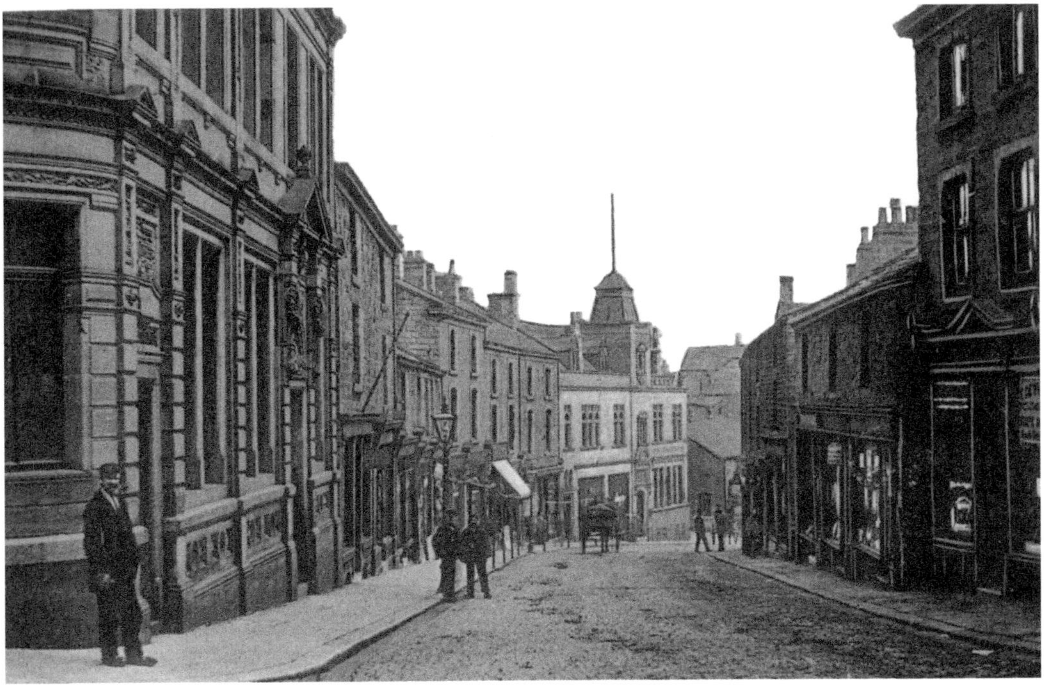

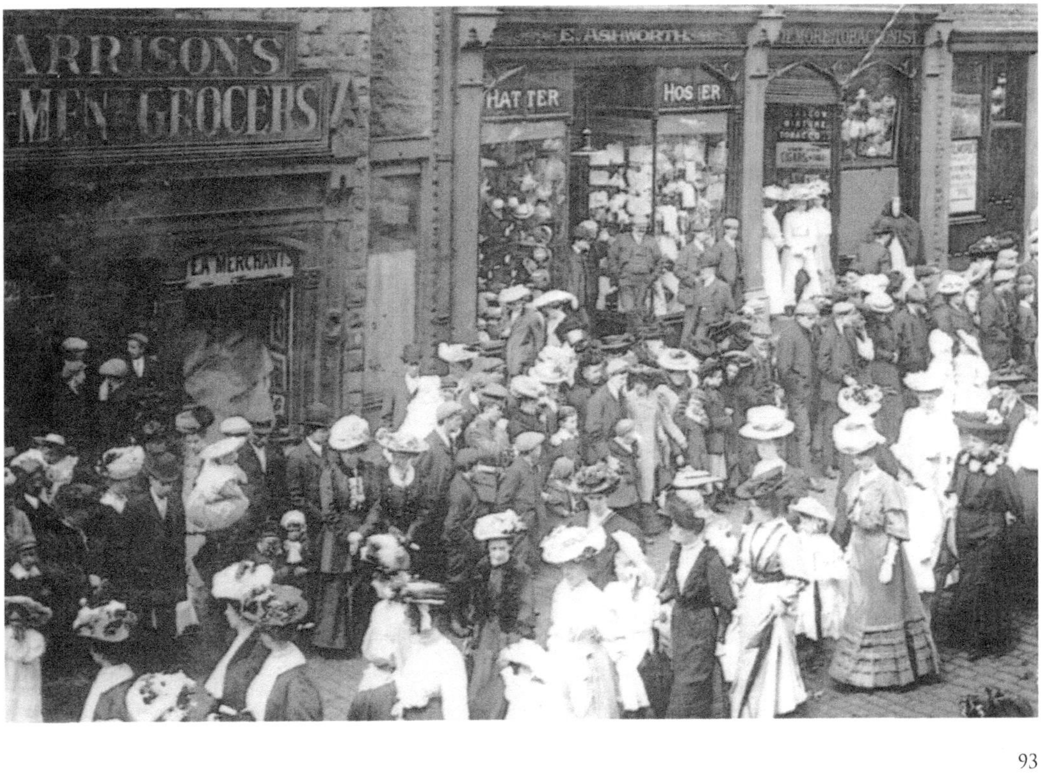
ARRISON'S
MEN GROCERS
E. ASHWORTH
HATTER
EA MERCHANTS

This church procession of 1910 is making its way in the opposite direction up Church Street across from Bank Street. The background is often as interesting as the foreground in images like these. On the immediate left is Trevelyan House and the Cross Hill Tavern. On the gable end there is an advert for Thomas Marsden, a piano and organ dealer who lived at 9 Blackburn Road and had a shop at 65 Church Street. (Ann Whalley)

Opposite above: We finish the book with this scene, which records a fund-raising day back in 1915, possibly for the war effort, outside St Leonard's Church. Tradition has it that the lady seated on the left-hand side was a Belgium refugee. Can anyone shed any more light on this photograph? (Ann Whalley)

Opposite below: It appears that there was no particular or special occasion for this photograph taken on St Giles Street around 1909 – a photographer happened to be passing by and just gathered a group of residents together and took this shot. It is not the most inspiring of images though, there are no smiles from the children, or the adults, but then these were hard times. It might seem obvious that the fellow sitting in the front row is one of the Padiham colliers, but then again he could be a local chimney sweep! (Ann Whalley)

95

Other titles published by The History Press

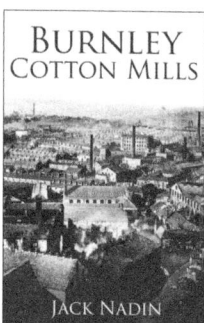

Burnley Cotton Mills
JACK NADIN

Burnley was once the cotton weaving capital of the world. In 1929, 63 per cent of the working population of Burnley was involved in the industry. This fascinating work illustrated with over ninety images, explores the history of this industry which was so central to the economy of Burnley. The author includes detailed histories of the 140 mill of Burnley, as well as stories of the weavers themselves and their families.

978 0 7524 4659 2

Burnley Inns and Taverns
JACK NADIN

This catalogue of the inns and taverns of Burnley provides a fascinating insight into the history of a town that was once considered 'the cotton capital of the world'. From the time when factory workers first crowded into squalid slum accommodation, these drinking establishments have been the setting for the most vibrant life of the town. With excerpts from local newspaper reports, this book will appeal to any reader with an interest in Burnley's forgotten past.

978 0 7524 4413 0

East Lancashire Mining Memories
JACK NADIN

The Lancashire Coalfield has all but gone, with little evidence of the industry apart from the memories of those who worked in it. Jack Nadin has gathered together the memories of many ex-miners. What was it like to work underground? What dangers lay down the mine? These questions and many more are answered by the men who did what was once Britain's most dangerous job, where the risk of death was high. Covering the area around Bury, Bolton, Clitheroe, Rawtenstall and Layton le Moors, this book is a reminder of the legacy of King Coal.

978 0 7524 4624 0

A Century of Burnley
CHRIS MAKEPEACE

This book offers an insight into the daily lives and living conditions of local people and gives the reader glimpses of familiar places during a century of unprecedented change. Many aspects of Burnley's recent history are covered, famous occasions and individuals are remembered, and the impact of national and international events is witnessed. This book recalls what Burnley has lost in terms of buildings, traditions and ways of life. It also acknowledges the regeneration that has taken place and celebrates the character and energy of local people.

978 0 7509 4916 3

Visit our website and discover thousands of other History Press books.

www.thehistorypress.co.uk

The History Press